Reptiles
Snapping Turtles

by Elizabeth Thomas

Consulting Editor: Gail Saunders-Smith, PhD

Content Consultant: Tanya Dewey, PhD
University of Michigan Museum of Zoology

CAPSTONE PRESS
a capstone imprint

Pebble Plus is published by Capstone Press,
151 Good Counsel Drive, P.O. Box 669, Mankato, Minnesota 56002.
www.capstonepub.com

 Books published by Capstone Press are manufactured with paper
containing at least 10 percent post-consumer waste.

Library of Congress Cataloging-in-Publication Data
Thomas, Elizabeth, 1953–
  Snapping turtles / by Elizabeth Thomas.
    p. cm.—(Pebble plus. Reptiles)
  Includes bibliographical references and index.
  Summary: "Simple text and photographs present Snapping Turtles, how they look, where they live, and what
they do"—Provided by publisher.
  ISBN 978-1-4296-6644-2 (library binding)
  1. Snapping turtles—Juvenile literature. I. Title.
  QL666.C539T46 2012
  597.92'2—dc22
                              2011002112

Editorial Credits
Lori Shores, editor; Gene Bentdahl, designer; Laura Manthe, production specialist

Photo Credits
Alamy: Bill Brooks, 15, imagebroker/Anton Luhr, 5; AnimalsAnimals: Breck P. Kent, 13; Getty Images Inc.: Danita
Delimont/Gallo Images, front cover, National Geographic/Bill Curtsinger, 9, Visuals Unlimited/Jim Merli, 11;
iStockphoto: Kent Allison, 7, back cover; Shutterstock: Gerald A. DeBoer, 1; Super Stock Inc./Animals Animals, 19, 21

Note to Parents and Teachers

The Reptiles set supports science standards related to life science. This book describes and
illustrates snapping turtles. The images support early readers in understanding the text. The
repetition of words and phrases helps early readers learn new words. This book also introduces
early readers to subject-specific vocabulary words, which are defined in the Glossary section.
Early readers may need assistance to read some words and to use the Table of Contents,
Glossary, Read More, Internet Sites, and Index sections of the book.

Printed in the United States of America in North Mankato, Minnesota.
032011
006110CGF11

Table of Contents

Snap!

Snapping turtles are too big
to hide in their shells.
But these turtles can bite
as fast as snakes.

Up Close!

Snapping turtles grow

from 8 to 15 inches

(20 to 38 centimeters) long.

Their shells are black,

brown, or dark green.

Snapping turtles have
strong jaws and long claws.
They have pointy scales
along their tails.

Watery Homes

Snapping turtles live
in ponds, marshes,
lakes, and streams.
They can stay underwater
for three hours.

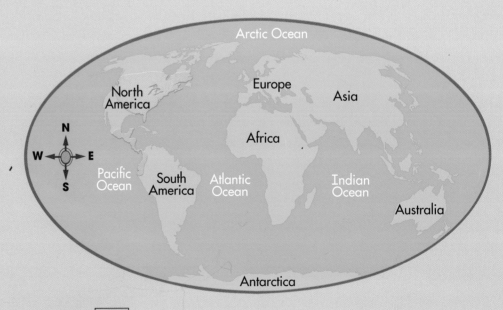

where snapping turtles live

A snapping turtle hunts
by hiding in mud.
It waits for fish, frogs,
or bugs to pass by. Snap!
The turtle grabs the prey.

In winter, snapping turtles

hibernate in soft mud.

They can go without food

for months.

From Egg to Turtle

Female snapping turtles

lay from 14 to 83 eggs.

They bury the leathery eggs

to keep them safe.

Snapping Turtle Life Cycle

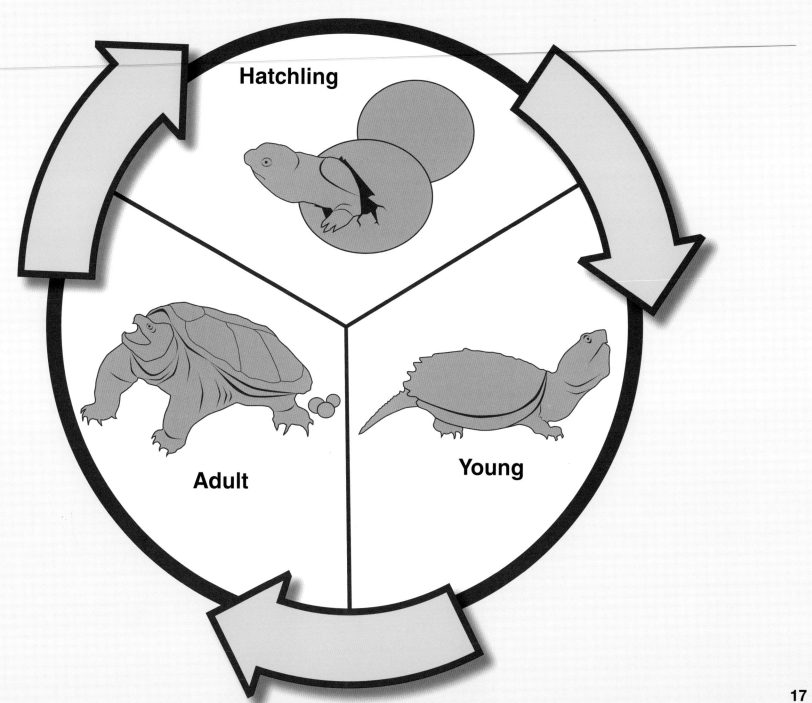

Hatchling

Young

Adult

Young snapping turtles

hatch from the eggs.

They are the size of quarters.

The little turtles begin

hunting right away.

Large birds, raccoons, and foxes eat young turtles. Snapping turtles that stay safe can live 30 to 40 years.

Glossary

hatch—to come out of an egg

hibernate—to spend winter in a deep sleep; animals hibernate to survive low temperatures and lack of food

leathery—having a rough, hard texture that is still flexible like leather

marsh—an area of wet, low land where grasses grow

prey—an animal eaten by another animal for food

scale—one of the small pieces of hard skin that cover the body of a reptile

Read More

Bredeson, Carmen. *Fun Facts about Turtles!* I Like Reptiles and Amphibians! Berkeley Heights, N.J.: Enslow Elementary, 2008.

Dickmann, Nancy. *A Turtle's Life.* Watch It Grow. Chicago: Heinemann Library, 2011.

Harris, Tim, editor. *Turtles.* Slimy, Scaly, Deadly Reptiles and Amphibians. New York: Gareth Stevens Pub., 2010.

Internet Sites

FactHound offers a safe, fun way to find Internet sites related to this book. All of the sites on FactHound have been researched by our staff.

Here's all you do:

Visit *www.facthound.com*

Type in this code: 9781429666442

Super-cool stuff! Check out projects, games and lots more at **www.capstonekids.com**

Index

Word Count: 167

Grade: 1

Early-Intervention Level: I